Obsessions: He

Copyright 2017 by W.R. Harris. All rights reserved.

You can check out all my writing, watch my videos, sign up for my newsletter, and receive a free download of one of my booksat www.wrhwriting.com

Or, check out my Facebook page: https://www.facebook.com/WRHarrisAuthor/

Chapter 1 1
Chapter 2 9
Chapter 3 18
Chapter 4 25
Chapter 5 37
Chapter 6 40
Chapter 7 49
Chapter 8 61
Chapter 9 68
Chapter 10 75
Afterword 77
About the Author 80

But go to Him when your need is desperate, when all other help is vain, and what do you find? A door slammed in your face, and a sound of bolting and double bolting on the inside. After that, silence. – C.S. Lewis, *A Grief Observed*

Chapter 1

What if I've blasphemed the Holy Spirit?

But I didn't actually say anything. Those were just involuntary thoughts.

But I said something bad about the Holy Spirit. Doesn't matter if it was just in my head. I still did it. Jesus said there's no forgiving that.

That's ridiculous. I know I'm God's child. End of discussion.

But what if? I mean, I did it. I can't deny that. Doesn't matter if it was involuntary thoughts. I still did it.

I feel a pang of anxiety. Thoughts whirl around my head so intensely I can hardly focus on what's in front of me. I get up off the couch and start walking around. Maybe that'll make the thoughts go away.

All right, I'm going to end this now. I'm God's child; he says there's no condemnation for me.

But what if?

No.

What if?

Another pang.

God damn the Holy Spirit. The Holy Spirit is Satan.

I did it now. If I wasn't guilty before, I am now.

But...

He said there's no forgiveness if I do that. Jesus doesn't lie.

But he promises.

He also says there's no forgiveness for that.

He promises never to leave his sheep. He promises he'll take anyone who comes to him.

But what if? What if I did it? I'll never know for sure. Not until I die, at least.

This is ridiculous. I'm not going to think about this.

I get up, take a shower, then go to bed.

***

My alarm wakes me up. I lay in bed for another minute or two while my mind adjusts to the reality of morning. All of a sudden, I feel anxious and the thoughts from yesterday come rushing back.

I'm never going to know for sure. My whole life will be spent wondering whether it's true. What if I did it?

I let that thought pass as best I can without challenging it. I go to the bathroom, eat breakfast, then hop on my bike to go to class. But on my way, I hear whispers in my head.

I gotta think about this. What if I did it?

The exercise from the bike ride helps clear my mind. I feel good when I walk into class. I sit down, get out my notebook, and prepare for the morning lecture.

"Zdravstvuyte! Kak dela?" my professor bellows. This is Russian class. I'm in the second semester, and I love it.

"Khorosho," most of the class replies.

My professor jokes around for a minute and then addresses some logistical business.

"Let's address some new adjectives because God knows we can't just say Khoroshii all the time. For instance, when something is rea..." *But what if I did it? I gotta think about it.*

I try to muster the energy to pay attention to class and forget my thoughts, but they're too strong. They're all I can hear. It feels as though they're pulling me down like I'm chained to an anchor. I try to stay above water, but I can't.

Why won't these thoughts go away? No, I didn't do it. Why can't I believe that and go on with my life?

What if I did it, though? I blasphemed the Holy Spirit. I can't debate that.

Sweat begins to build on my palms and my chest tightens.

Face it. I did it. I'm going to hell forever.

Maybe I did. Maybe it's true. What if I am? This is hell. I'm already in hell. I can't live like this. I didn't do it. I know I didn't. Jesus said there's no condemnation for those in Christ. But what if I did it? He promised to accept everyone who comes to him but he also promises to never accept the one who commits the unpardonable sin. I'm never going to know which category I belong to until I die. Until then I'll spend the rest of my life wondering. How am I going to live like that? I can't live like that. And these thoughts won't seem to go away. My other obsessive thoughts would go away because they weren't that big of a deal but hell forever is a big deal so that's something I can't just forget about and how would I get rid of these thoughts when even talking about them to someone probably won't make much of a difference what else is there to do my life is over I mean how am I going to function.

There's a knot in my stomach. I feel like I'm going to throw up. I take a deep breath and focus in on class.

"Tak, skazhitye pozhaluysta…"

The anchor starts dragging me down again. I try to stay above water. But human strength has about a zero percent chance of overcoming the weight of an anchor.

My stomach and chest are tightening so much I'm starting to panic. Deep breaths, deep breaths deep breaths deep breaths deep breaths.

Let's think about this.

Deep breaths deep breaths deep breaths.

"Otlichna! Ross, what would you say if you went to a restaurant and the food was really good?"

"Ochen vkusnii," I reply.

"Khorosho, khorosho. Blake, what would you say…"

Focus on breathing. If I just focus on breathing, I can calm down. Then class will be over and I can get on my bike, which will make me feel better.

***

Class dismissed. I walk to my bike and pedal home. Fresh air, going fast, my heart beating from the exercise and the anxiety, the sweat from the Texas humidity and heat—it all makes me feel better. But I know it won't last long. I try to enjoy it while it does. I know the oppression is coming.

I unlock my apartment door and walk in. The light from the windows is the only light. Doesn't seem like anyone's home. I catch my breath for a second. To my right, my eyes hook onto a set of green books on my bookshelf. They are a collection of Charles Spurgeon's sermons I bought online several years ago. I try to not to look.

Spurgeon would condemn me.

I put my bike up. I want to study for a bit and eat lunch.

He'd condemn me.

I try not to even look in the direction of the books. I'm paralyzed.

Go study. Walk in your room and study.

But I need to think about this.

Go study. C'mon.

I start toward my room, but anxious pressure shoots throughout my body causing me to stop after one step. I stand still.

I gotta go sit on the couch and think about this.

My brain is telling me to go to my room. Everything else in my body is screaming desperately to sit on the couch and think. Almost involuntarily, I walk to the couch. I sit staring at the books.

Spurgeon talks about the sweetness and compassion of Jesus. He believed Jesus didn't let go of his sheep.

He talks about sinners and damnation, though. If he knew what I did he'd yell me to perdition in classic fire-and-brimstone fashion.

It doesn't matter what Spurgeon thinks. He'd probably tell me I'm one of Christ's sheep, but even if he didn't it only matters what Jesus says, and he accepts everyone who comes to him.

Cool. Case closed.

I try to sit up. The anxious weight pushes me back on the couch.

I can do this. Jesus help me do this.

I try again. Same result.

Deep breaths, deep breaths. C'mon!

I get up.

Not done thinking about this. Sit back down.

I force myself to walk to my room and throw myself on my bed.

I feel insane. I'm a normal person, though. Why is this happening to me? I've never done drugs in my life. I've never even touched alcohol. People like me. I go to church. I share the gospel. I serve at church. I don't just pretend to be Christian. I have a great family. I'm not mentally ill. I'm not schizophrenic. I played football. I was prom king at my high school. I make good grades. I graduated high school. I go to a prestigious university. I have a 4.0 average four semesters into college. What the heck? What the heck?

I lay there for a minute and just breathe.

I've got stuff to do. Jeez, this sucks. How am I supposed to function? Why can't I just function like a normal person? I used to be able to. Why can't I focus on small, everyday tasks?

I can't focus while I'm cooking, I can't focus on watching T.V., I can't focus on reading, which is something I used to love.

Tears well up in my eyes.

I just want to be a normal person.

I shake my head to force back the tears.

I need to take a shower. I can do this.

I jump up from my bed, grab some clean clothes, and head to the bathroom. I start the shower and wait for it to warm up.

I feel a shot of anxiety. *Did I do it?*

No, don't think about it.

I try to let the thought go. For a fleeting second, I feel relieved. Then, the anxiety doubles. I put my forearm against the wall of the shower and lay my head on it.

Don't think about it, don't think about it.

My head feels as though it's about to burst. My whole body seems to tighten, especially my arms.

My blood pressure must be through the roof. My body can't keep handling this. I'm going to die soon. My life is over.

The steady sound of the water on the shower tile reminds me of the task at hand.

I'm wasting water. I need to get in.

I lift my head off my forearm. My head feels like an anchor slowly dragging me towards the bottom of the sea. I lay my head back on my forearm.

I'm going to die soon and go to hell forever. I just need to accept it.

A tear flows out of my left eye and quickly pools on my forearm. I can't resist the tears anymore; they flow freely now as I start to sob silently. My whole body shakes uncontrollably.

"Why, God?" I say in a shaky voice. "Why would you do this to me?"

I'm so confused, and I'm mad at him. *Why would he put me through this?* Never in my life have I told God I hate him, but I want to right now.

I'll go to hell forever if I say I hate him.

What does it matter? I'm going to hell forever anyway.

"I hate you. I hate you."

Chapter 2

The train keeps chugging along. Chug, chug, chug. All around the train it's dark. The train keeps chugging and it stays dark. No light, no light. Where's the light? Where's the light?

My eyes open and I stare at the ceiling. *Will there ever be light?*

My chest tightens with anxiety. Desperate to find some relief, I reach over for my pen and journal. "*I have no relief from my fear,*" I scribble.

I need to study. I muster all my energy to get out of bed and sit at my desk. I reach for my Russian book. *Did I do it? Am I guilty? I need to think about this.* My hand stops in midair.

Just pick up the book.

I reach toward the book.

I need to think. I need to think.

I pick up the book anyway. I flip to the page I need and start reading, all the while ignoring my thoughts. I answer the first question, then the second. My brain already feels tired.

I can't go on. Jeez, I can't go on any further. I need a break.

I stop and breathe for about a minute and try to ignore everything going on in my head.

All right now. Focus.

I answer another question, and then I struggle to answer one more.

I'm guilty. I'm going to hell forever.

I can't stand this anymore. I gotta go watch T.V. and forget about everything.

I walk over to the living room, plop on the couch, and turn on the television. Basketball's on.

Please, Jesus. Take my anxiety away.

It's deep in the second half, and it's a good game. A player makes a jumper to tie it up with 50 seconds to go.

All those theologians–what would they say? Would they confirm that I'm guilty? C.S. Lewis talks about the grace of Jesus, but he also talks about sins and damnation. Jonathan Edwards believed in the security of salvation, but he also shouted about sinners in the hands of an angry God. I think they and any other reasonable pastor would console my anxiety and tell me of Jesus's grace, but they don't know the severity of the names I've called him. If they did, would they potentially tell me they're not sure what my fate is?

Forget about it. Just focus on the game.

I focus on the game for about a minute and a half. But then the anxiety builds up. My stomach feels slightly sick, and my head feels so much pressure that I think my skull's going to cave in. I try to avoid thinking about my worries, but I can't. The floodgates open.

I'm going to hell forever.

My palms get sweaty and my heart races.

There's nothing I can do about it.

Tears come to my eyes.

This can't be right. I know deep down it's not right. Why can't I believe? Help my unbelief.

But I still feel just as anxious.

***

I take a shower and walk back to my bedroom. The overhead light is turned off; my roommate has his lamp on and is reading. I get in bed.

Should I journal tonight? I don't really feel like it.

I flip my covers on top of me and close my eyes.

Surely that's not what Jesus means when he says that. Surely he doesn't mean that if you think a bad thought about the Holy Spirit you're damned forever. That contradicts everything else he teaches. He says multiple times those who come to him will never be cast out.

But I literally blasphemed the Holy Spirit. I can't say I didn't. How can I argue I didn't do it?

I've been over this a million times. I didn't do it. Stop thinking, brain. Stop thinking and go to sleep.

I successfully prevent my brain from thinking for five seconds.

But what if??

Stop. Please stop.

But what if?? I have to think about this. I have to convince myself it's not true. Jesus says those who believe have eternal life!

Except those who've blasphemed the Holy Spirit, which I can't truthfully argue I haven't done.

Paul says there's no condemnation for those who are in Christ Jesus.

But is someone who's blasphemed the Holy Spirit in Christ Jesus? If I'm not in Christ, I don't have that protection. And if I blasphemed the Holy Spirit, there's no possible way I can be in Christ.

I clench my teeth and turn over. *Stop thinking! Just stop thinking!*

I reach over to my desk and pick up my iPod. *Maybe some music will help me fall asleep.* I put my earbuds in and turn it to my favorite song.

Give it three or four songs. Then, I'll fall asleep.

I listen to the music, my head still on my pillow and my thoughts still racing.

Two songs...three songs...four...five...six.

This isn't working. My head's still spinning like crazy.

I turn off my iPod and set it back on my desk. I stare at the ceiling. *Surely there's something about fear of the unpardonable sin on a counseling website. Surely someone else has gone through this.*

I look over to my roommate. His open book covers his face and he's snoring. I reach over to the middle of my desk and pick up my laptop. I type in a search for Christian counseling and blasphemy against the Holy Spirit. I come across a good-looking Christian counseling website and find two hits for anxiety and blasphemy against the Spirit. The article details how the gist of Jesus' comment is targeted toward unbelievers who reject him. He's not cautioning believers to make sure they never accidentally commit it...Jesus loves his children unconditionally...Not once in the Gospels does Jesus reject someone who comes to him...If you're concerned, you can be sure you probably haven't committed it.

Probably?

My chest and arms tighten, and my head feels like an anvil. *What if I did it, though? I'm not going to know for sure until I die.*

I know I haven't rejected Jesus. As the guy says, Jesus never rejects those who come to him. The counselor guy says I'm fine.

Probably? That's a lot of assurance for people who are worried they're damned forever with no way to reverse it. Probably? What kind of bull crap is that? This counselor guy should know better! Now I'm really never going to fall asleep.

I turn my laptop off and set it back on my desk. I sit up in my bed and stare at the wall, the same debate playing over and over in my head. *Stop thinking, just stop thinking about this... But I need to think. If I can just go through everything in my head one more time, I can really convince myself I'm saved... Jesus never forsakes his children; there is no condemnation for those in him... Except I blasphemed the Holy Spirit. There's no forgiveness, there's no forgiveness... I'll never know for sure until I die... Until then, I live in anxiety.*

Desperate for some kind of release, I grab my pen and my small black journal.

"Help me, God. Help me help me help me help me help me help me. Things just seem to get worse and worse. I need you. Save me from the hell I create for myself."

I look at my clock. It's 1:35am, an hour and a half since I first tried to go to sleep. My mind is fried, and I feel a tiny glimmer of sleepiness. *Please let me go to sleep.* I lay my head on my pillow. Five minutes later, I fall asleep.

***

I lock my truck and start walking to the gym where church service is. Bunches of college students in groups walk alongside me. I feel like a big chunk of heavy lead.

Hopefully church will make me feel better. Jesus loves me, this I know...

But he also doesn't forgive the unpardonable sin. All sins will be forgiven them, including any blasphemies they utter. But the sin against the Holy Spirit will never be forgiven. I've blasphemed the Holy Spirit. Judgment, damnation, God's wrath—that's my portion.

Just keep walking. Maybe something in church will stick. Maybe something will make me feel better.

I walk up the stairs toward the gym. As I approach, I see my friend Sean talking with two other guys.

"Hey, Ross, what's up?"

My head hurts. It takes every ounce of mental energy to focus on him and not my thoughts. "Hey, man. How are you?"

"I'm great. I haven't seen you in a few weeks. How've things been going?"

"Uh, pretty good," I say as I nod my head, almost to convince myself my answer is truthful.

That's a lie.

I continue, "You know, just really busy with homework. Russian class is a lot of work."

"I bet, dude. Sounds like a lot. I don't know how you do that."

I chuckle. "Yeah, sometimes I'm not sure how I do it either."

"We'll have to grab something to eat soon."

"For sure. That'd be great."

"All right. I'll text you sometime this week."

"Sounds good. Good to see you."

"You too, man."

I walk into the gym and find a seat. People are still standing around talking. Service hasn't started.

I feel bad lying about how I'm doing. I don't know what else to say, though. "Well, no, actually I'm not doing well. I'm going to hell forever for committing the unpardonable sin. I'm more stressed than I've ever been, and I don't know what to do. If you can help me, please do."

The band walks on stage. "How are y'all doing tonight?" the worship leader asks. The audience cheers in response. "Good. Let's worship Jesus."

Everyone stands for worship. The band starts with a familiar tune. I know the words that come next. I sing along. "Je-eee-sus. The healer of brokenness. Sa-aaav-ior. The fixer of troubled souls."

My spirit feels slightly lifted as I sing. *Is he strong enough to fix my troubled soul? I hope he is; I think he is. How could anyone get out of the hole I'm in? Just keep praying. Just keep trying. I don't feel like there's hope, but maybe there is somehow. I'll find out.*

Worship makes me feel better. I hope the sermon will too.

Worship ends, the audience sits, and one of the pastors gives announcements. The lead pastor replaces him, prays, and opens his Bible.

"Today's text is…"

Immediately, I feel heavy and tight all over. I bow my head towards the ground. I can't bring myself to look at him while he reads the text.

Help me, God. I want to love your word. It just feels like condemnation to me.

I try as hard as I can to resist the anxiety that is ready to bust down the door. It creeps in slowly anyway. By the third minute of the sermon, my head feels ready to burst.

Just keep breathing, just keep breathing.

"God hates sin. It's obvious from the text. The result of sin is eternal separation from God. Church, we need to realize the pernicious effects of sin in our lives and work to eradicate it."

Sin has taken over my life. I've lost the battle. Eternal, irreversible separation from God. That's the result.

My head and chest feel so tight that I just want to jump up and run out of the gym. I fidget in my seat.

"But friends, here's the good news. God took out his wrath on Jesus so he doesn't have to do it to us. Jesus is the substitute. If you believe in Jesus, you don't have to worry about God's wrath. It's been satisfied in Jesus' sacrifice. If you believe in Jesus, you live with God now and for life everlasting. You are God's child, and nothing can take you away from him."

Except if you blaspheme the Holy Spirit. I am the exception. I am the sheep that God lost. He will never take me back.

"Believe that today, church. Take comfort in his grace. Find joy in him, and use it to pursue holiness."

I'll try to pursue holiness, but God still won't take me back.

The pastor ends his sermon. I feel like I'm about to go insane, throw up, and have a heart attack all at the same time. I put my head in my palms and fight back tears.

Thank God he's praying. People won't be able to see me losing my mind.

The band starts playing again. Everyone around me stands. For a second, I can't bring myself to move, so I pray.

I'm exhausted, God. I can barely focus on anything except my thoughts. Heal me. Do something. I'm tired of this.

I stand up for the last worship song. Service ends, which relieves me. I'm able to move and get my mind off God's wrath dragging me to hell.

Chapter 3

I can't do this. It's been three weeks since this started, and I can't focus on my homework anymore, I can't focus in class no matter how hard I try, it takes every ounce of energy to get out of bed in the morning, I can't fall asleep at night, my grades are plummeting, I feel like I'm going to have a heart attack, I can't even focus on conversations with my roommates, going to church makes me feel worse because I feel God's judgment weigh me down every second I'm there.

I sit in bed thinking and staring at the ceiling. My eyes see the ceiling, but my brain is focused on my thoughts.

Thank God I have today off. I'm going to chill for a bit. I'll study for my Russian final later.

My phone rings.

Who's calling me?

I pick up.

"Hello?"

"Ross, it's Megan. Where are you?"

"What?"

"You're supposed to be taking the Russian final right now! It started thirty minutes ago. You weren't here, so I asked to go to the bathroom so I could call you."

"I thought the final was scheduled for Saturday."

"No, it's today. Come over here now!"

"Coming."

My heart is already racing. I click off the phone and hurriedly put clothes on. I grab my bike and fly out the front door. Once I get on the road, I race down the street and down the hill towards class. I get as close as I can to the building housing my final, throw my bike on a bike rack, and fumble with the lock. I sprint up another hill, throw open the heavy door to the building and take two steps with each stride up the stairs. I open the classroom door, sweaty and out of breath, and half the class looks up at me from their tests. My professor motions at me to just take a seat. I do and the T.A. hands me the test. I take a second to catch my breath.

I can't believe I just did this. I've never straight up misheard a test date, especially a final. He's bound to have said it multiple times. I was trying to pay attention. How did I not know it was today?

I take a few seconds to try and get over my mistake. But I'm mad at myself.

This is embarrassing. I can't believe I did this.

Despite my mind protesting to keep thinking about how upset I am, I open the test and start working. Not long after I start, the first person leaves. And then several leave. All of a sudden, I'm working with one other person in the room. Somehow, I finish before her, and I hand my test to the T.A. I'm somewhat relieved the other girl is still in there because otherwise I'd probably have to explain why I was so late. I walk down the stairs shaking my head, still in disbelief I was so convinced the final was scheduled for Saturday.

Thankfully I studied some the past two days. I don't feel like I did too bad. That could've been much worse. But still, how did I do that?

***

I pedal back to my apartment, my mind still buzzing with confusion and anger. I open the door, set my bike against the wall, and walk to my room. I throw my backpack on my bed in frustration, not realizing my roommate is sitting on his bed reading.

"Bad day?" he says.

I shake my head. "I had my Russian final today. I thought it was tomorrow. Megan called me thirty minutes into it to ask where the heck I was."

"That sucks. Did you bomb it?"

"I don't know. I actually think I did okay."

"Why'd you think it was tomorrow?"

I shake my head again. "I don't know. I haven't been sleeping in class. I thought I was paying attention. I could've sworn he said multiple times it was Saturday. I've never done anything like that before."

"Well, at least you didn't miss it."

"Yeah. No joke."

I sit at my desk chair and exhale. I stare at the wall for a second.

"You all right?" my roommate asks.

"Dude, I can't...I can't do this anymore. I can't live like this."

"What do you mean?"

"I've been struggling with depression on and off for the past several years. I've just been dealing with it, and I've made it through okay. But I'm tired of living like this. I can't do my

20

homework, my grades are falling, I can't concentrate on anything, I have very little energy, it takes me forever to do anything."

"I noticed you seem down the past few weeks."

"And I keep having thoughts that I've committed the unpardonable sin. You know what I'm referring to?"

"Yeah, I think so."

"I know it's ridiculous. I just can't get it out of my head."

We sit in silence for a few seconds.

"So, what are you going to do?" my roommate asks. He's a proactive type.

"I've been thinking about going to Recovery on Monday nights at church. I keep thinking I should do it, and I never do it. I'll go Monday."

"All right. I'm holding you to it."

***

I jump in my truck, a little nervous about the journey ahead.

I gotta try something. I gotta start somewhere.

As I'm driving I feel relief that I'm finally taking this first step, but I'm also nervous it won't help.

Gotta try something.

I park, get out of my truck, walk to the church, and open the door.

I don't know anybody who's going to be in that room.

I walk into the room. There's about 25 people. I don't know anyone. Everyone is standing around the room in groups talking. I take a seat in one of the chairs that's been set out. I sit for a few minutes by myself, and then someone stands at the front of the room and calls for attention. Everyone takes a seat.

"Welcome to Recovery. We're glad you're here this evening. We'll break into small groups in a minute, but first I want to remind everyone that we're here for each other, to listen to each other, not to judge, not to necessarily delve into all the details, not to try to counsel each other. Like I said, we're here to just listen and support each other. For those maybe here for the first time, we don't share who we're seeing for counseling or make any recommendations for counseling. We have books on the table in the back. We recommend those books. They're all available on the internet. So, guys will break into small groups on this side of the room; girls will go to that side. Find three or four people sitting next to you and make a group."

I look around and make eye contact with two guys sitting next to each other. They motion to me and one other guy and ask, "You guys want to join us?"

"Yeah," I respond.

"Sure," says the other guy.

We move our chairs into a small circle.

"How y'all doing?" one of the guys asks.

"All right. How are y'all?" I say.

"Not bad, not bad. So, what do you say we get started? If it's okay with y'all, I'll go first."

He describes what he's going through. We listen, and when he's done his friend and the other guy in the group give him brief encouragement. The other two guys do the same, and those listening offer encouragement. They look at me to indicate it's my turn.

"Well, I've been struggling kind of on and off for the past several years with depression. I've just lived with it and pushed through it and done okay. I've wanted sometimes to try and get help, but I didn't know how to go about it. Things have gotten worse lately, though, and I knew I had to do something to try to get better, so I figured I'd try Recovery. I don't know what my next steps are, but I have supportive small group leaders at church and a supportive roommate. So, I'm just trying to start this process of finally doing something to get better."

"Thanks for sharing, man," the other guys say.

"Thanks for coming," one says. "Just keep at it."

We sit quietly while the two friends chat for about a minute. Then the guy from the beginning gets up at the front and calls for attention. We all move our chairs back into rows and listen.

"Is there anyone here tonight who is here for the first time?" he asks.

I raise my hand along with two others.

"So, to celebrate your starting this journey, come up to the front, and I'll give you one of these coins."

I walk up to him, and he hands me a plastic blue coin. On one side is written "Grace for this journey." On the other is written 2 Corinthians 12:9: "My grace is sufficient for you, for my power is made perfect in weakness."

I thank him and sit down. After a few more orders of business, he dismisses us. I walk back to my truck and start driving

23

home. I feel good for finally taking the first step, but the meeting didn't help as much as I wanted it to.

Why don't they want people recommending counselors? That's what I think I need and I don't know where or how to find one.

Chapter 4

I sit down at the edge of my bed.

What if North Korea bombs us? What if it happens?

My chest and throat tighten.

I'm going to feel a blast and then I'm going to die.

It's fine. Nothing bad is going to happen. Everything's okay.

But what if?

Tears well up in my eyes.

I don't have any control over this. I wish I had control. Then I wouldn't have to worry. Mom and Dad are downstairs. We just played board games. They aren't concerned about this. I shouldn't be either.

But what if? Whatifwhatifwhatif?

***

I sit at my desk in English class. I bend down and grab my book and my journal for the start of class. As I reach back up toward my desk, the big gash on my elbow from yesterday's football game brushes against the side of the desk. I wince a little and put my books on the desk.

What if someone else touched the desk with an open wound right where I did? What if I just contracted AIDS?

I don't think that's how it works.

But if someone's open wound did touch right there... What if they had AIDS? If the virus is there, wouldn't I catch it?

I'm already exhausted from the football game. My head feels heavy. I put my head in my hands for a second to rest.

"Are you okay, Ross?" my teacher asks.

I lift my head quickly. "Yes ma'am, I'm fine. Just tired from yesterday's game."

"I imagine you are," she says sweetly.

I may have just gotten AIDS.

I'm too tired to even concern myself with the thought further. But I know it'll come back, even though I don't want it to.

***

I wake up. My body and my head feel slightly tight.

I just woke up. Why am I anxious?

I open my eyes a little wider and look around.

I have AIDS.

My head hurts just from the anticipation of what's coming.

No, no. Why? Why is this going on? Why won't it go away?

26

I'm going to die in the coming years. There's nothing I can do about it.

I wish I hadn't touched that stupid desk. Then this wouldn't be happening to me. Why won't these thoughts go away? Just go away.

My alarm goes off again.

I gotta get ready for school.

But all I want to do is sit here and cry.

***

I gotta be the best. Nobody else works as hard as me. I'm going to be the best football player on my team. In three years, I'm going to receive scholarship offers. I'm going to play Division One college football. I can't waste a day. I can't waste a minute. That's my motto. If I'm not working out, I'll be watching highlight videos of college recruits online. No one works harder than me.

Someone knocks on my bedroom door. "Hey, man, you want to work out at T.J.'s today?" my brother asks.

I pop up from my chair and head over to my dresser for my workout clothes. "Yeah," I respond.

Yeah, I'm dead tired from working out all week. But I work harder than anyone else. Plus, I'd feel lazy if I just sat at home. Can't have wasted time or else someone else might be getting better than me.

I put on my workout clothes and look at the clock. I still have an hour before we leave for workout.

Let's see. What can I do to be productive until workout?

Something in my head tells me I've already done pretty much everything I could do to learn about the game of football today. But I start listing everything off in my head anyway.

Did I watch highlights? Yes. Did I read up on offensive strategy and play-calling? Yes.

My head hurts. I've been studying all day.

Did I study some film of myself from last year? Yes.

I gotta do something productive, though. Doesn't matter if my brain hurts. I work harder than anyone else. I'll watch more highlights.

***

My brother starts the car. "Man, I hate having a black car," he says.

"Shoot, man. I'm already sweating bullets from practice," I reply. I wait for a few more seconds and then fall into the passenger seat.

"The seat is hot, but I don't care. My legs are dead," I remark.

We drive off. It's the normal drive home, but today I feel even more exhausted than usual.

I work my butt off. I work harder than just about anyone on the team. I should be proud to be tired.

But I don't feel proud. Today I just feel so exhausted. Tears well up in my eyes from the exhaustion.

I was tired last year, but I had friends who I could talk about football with and joke with. No other sophomores in my class care about football as much as I do, and they don't get my sense of humor.

The tears are almost coming out.

Dude, you're in the car with your brother after football practice. Man up.

I take some deep breaths to prevent my tears from coming. I feel a weird pit in my stomach. As we keep driving it gets worse. My brother is blasting the radio, which comforts me a little since it makes any distress I'm showing a little less noticeable. A song from his iPod ends and a new one begins.

Oh no. Not this song. Not right now.

The melancholy melody begins, and I frantically try to breathe deeply to prevent myself from crying.

Just get through this song and something more upbeat will come on.

The next song begins. *Thank God. This is better.*

I start singing along. The pit is still in my stomach.

***

I brush my teeth and then head to the bedroom. My brother is already on the bottom bunk playing on his phone. I climb the ladder to the top bunk and plop down.

Twenty minutes pass. I don't hear my brother anymore. I peep below and see he's asleep.

Is this my life now? I thought things would be better by now, but they aren't. Things just seem to be getting worse and worse. I don't connect with anyone here. I don't really have any friends. I feel like I'm about to burst, and I feel like my chest is an anchor. I can barely sit up.

Tears are coming. I try to stop them, but I can't. Two fall down my cheek, and then all of a sudden I'm blubbering. I try to stay silent. I don't want my brother to know I'm crying. A feeling of pure terror comes over me.

My life is over. Things are never going to get better.

The darkness of our room seems to grow darker. *There is no light in my life.* I feel myself shaking uncontrollably.

God, why are you doing this to me? I hate you. Why would you do this to me?

My weeping softens a little, but I still feel as though nothing but terror surrounds me.

"Oh, God," I whisper through my tears, "please help me. Please, Jesus. Please help me."

***

I look up at my alarm clock. It's 3:52 in the afternoon. *I've been laying here for the past twenty minutes just thinking. I should probably get up.*

I stay where I am, though.

God's gotten me through a lot. I went through that terrible time of depression in high school, and he got me through it. I didn't come all the way out of depression, but he brought me a good way out of it. I've always thought that if he could get

*me through that then he could get me through anything.
When this whole blaspheming the Holy Spirit thing started I
didn't think anything could get me out of it because I literally
thought God left me. I really did think I had no hope. But
maybe he can prove me wrong. Maybe he can get me out of
this too.*

I feel energized. I almost feel happy. "Wow," I whisper, "I
haven't felt this way in a while."

The feeling quickly dissipates, but a tiny bit of it stays with me.

Say it. Tell God you believe.

"God," I whisper again, "I believe you can heal me, so do it."

***

My phone rings.

"Hello?"

"Hi, is this Ross?"

"Yes."

"Hey, it's Sarah from the counseling office. So, I talked with
our supervisor and he said we can offer you counseling free of
charge since you're serving as an intern at church."

I breathe a sigh of relief. "Oh, thank God! Thanks for letting
me know."

"No problem!"

I put my phone down and breathe another sigh of relief.

"Who was that?" my roommate asks.

"The counseling office at the church. They said I don't have to pay for counseling, because I'm interning for the church right now. Thank God. I thought I was only going to be able to afford one or two sessions. They were about the cheapest counseling I could find, and I want to do it with Christian counselors."

"There you go. God's opening doors."

***

I walk up the stairs to the counseling office. I'm sweating and nervous. I open the door.

"Hi, are you here for an appointment?" The receptionist asks.

"Yes. 11:30."

She checks me in, and I sit down. *How do I tell my counselor that I'm terrified I'm going to hell? I guess I'm just going to have to spit it out.*

The door to the back rooms open. My counselor, who I recognize from the online profile, steps out.

"Ross?" she says.

"Hi, that's me," I say as I get up from my chair.

"Hi, nice to meet you," she says as she shakes my hand.

"You too."

We walk back to a room. "Have a seat on the sofa," she says as she closes the door behind us. I sit down as she gets settled in her chair across from me.

"So, tell me a little about yourself," she says.

"Well, my dad was in the military, so I lived all over the place when I was little. I grew up in a Christian household. We attended church regularly. I hated it, though. I thought church was boring, and I didn't understand what it meant to follow Jesus. We moved to Texas when I was in second grade, and then we moved here when I came into 10th grade. I had a difficult time transitioning to my new school. I didn't connect with my classmates very well, and I got really lonely. Things didn't seem to be getting better, so I fell into depression. I couldn't concentrate on anything, my grades plummeted, I felt sad all the time and I cried almost nightly before going to sleep, I had no energy. For the first time in my life, I started crying out to God. It was crazy and I can't really explain it, but over the course of a month God started changing me. I had a better attitude, I wanted to love other people and show them kindness, I told my classmates about how great God is, I had a desire to study the Bible and go to church."

"Wow. Sounds like God's done incredible things in your life," she interjects.

"Yeah, for sure. I transferred schools again my junior year. It took about a year, but I ended up loving that school. I led a Christian group on campus. I told people about Jesus—I followed him as hard as I could. Things had gotten better, but I still suffered from depression. I still felt exhausted all the time, I still had concentration problems, all that. I enjoyed the school more and I felt a lot of purpose in what I was doing for Jesus. So, I was able to push through my depression."

"Did you go to your doctor or get on any medication by this point?"

"No."

"So, you were able to just push through?"

"Yeah. I managed somehow."

She nods. "Okay. Go on."

"I went off to college in east Texas. I followed Jesus there—two of my friends and I started praying together first semester. We prayed for God to move on campus at that small school. By second semester, we built up a guys' Bible study group of about 11 guys. One of those guys began a weekly prayer night on campus, which reached a lot of people. God really moved there. With my friends and with the purpose and momentum of God's movement, I made it through the depression I still dealt with. Like my senior year of high school, I still had all the symptoms. I just dealt with it—I still didn't go to my doctor or receive medication."

"Wow. It must have been hard struggling through all that and still trying to function."

"It was. Harder than I can describe."

I pause, trying to fight away the tears that came with painful memories.

"Anyway, I transferred to school back here. I thought I was going to have the same sort of impact for the Kingdom that I did at my first college. I started out well. I made all A's in summer classes and for my first full semester. But the university is so big here. I've been trying to get plugged in somewhere and make friends. I haven't found somewhere I feel like I belong, though. I feel lonely again; I don't have the activity and the close friends to prop me up. So, this semester I became consumed by my depression. My grades plummeted, and I can barely function at all now. My parents are confused about what's going on."

"Have you ever considered going to your doctor to get on anti-depressants?"

"Kind of. I just…I'm one of those people who doesn't like to take medicine unless I absolutely have to."

"Well, I can tell you this. Some people are really helped by antidepressants. It's okay to take medicine. It's not a sin. I won't make any decisions for you, but it might help."

I nod. "Okay. I'll consider it."

"Do you journal?"

"Yeah, sometimes."

"Between now and the time we meet next week, try this. Read through some Psalms. Pray through them, and pray that God would help you believe in his love. Write down all your thoughts about the Psalm and write down your prayers. Pour out your heart before God. Tell him everything; hold nothing back."

"I'll do that."

"What is your goal for our time together?"

I think for a moment. "To get out of this funk. I know my depression may not go away; I just want to be able to function."

She nods and jots down a few notes on a notepad. "Okay. Think about visiting your doctor—if that's something you want to do or not. And try journaling. I think it may be the beginning of expressing your feelings to God and start the healing process. When we meet next week, we'll discuss how your journaling went."

"Sounds good."

She sets her notepad on the small table next to her and puts her hands together. "Is it okay if I pray?"

"Sure."

35

She begins her prayer. A tiny feeling of hope sparks within me.

But what if things never improve. What if this is my life?

Just keep going. Just keep trying.

"Amen."

"Amen."

I stand up and shake her hand. "Thanks for your time."

She smiles. "My pleasure. See you next week."

I walk out and say bye to the receptionist. I walk down the hallway to the stairs.

Why didn't I mention blasphemy against the Spirit?

I clinch my teeth in frustration.

I chickened out.

Chapter 5

After I finish my homework, I take a shower and come back to my bedroom. My roommate is still at work, so it's just me.

This is probably the best time I'll have to journal.

I put my massage cushion on my headrest and grab my pen and journal. I sit and stare at the wall.

I don't feel like writing. What do I even say?

I think about my counselor's words.

Don't hold anything back. Just write. Word vomit. Get it out.

I turn to the first blank page. I hesitate.

Don't think about it. Don't be a perfectionist. You don't have to write everything like a college English essay.

I start writing, not knowing where I'm going with it.

"I'm having a hard time believing you love me, Lord. I want more than anything to believe that, but I don't. I feel like you're incessantly mad at me for the things I've done, almost as though you hold a grudge against me for not obeying properly or for sinning a particular sin.

This is what I feel: abandonment, disappointment, disgust. I feel as though you search my heart and find egregious sin and are appalled at it. I committed the blasphemy against the Holy Spirit—the one thing that goes beyond the scope of ordinary sin. And now you can't stand me anymore. If you let me into heaven, you'll be unhappy about it, as though I was a disappointing child. I feel you're disgusted with me, and there's nothing that can be done about it.

I want to feel loved again. I hope it will happen. But my life is bleak. I think it'll be a long time before that changes. Help me somehow to hope and believe. Help me to feel love and joy again."

I look at my clock. 11:23pm. For the first time in the last two or three weeks, my mind feels somewhat relaxed before bed. I try my best to not think about anything. 15 minutes later, I fall asleep.

***

I turn off the overhead light, turn on my desk lamp, grab my Bible, and sit in bed.

God, I want to love your word. Help me not to be afraid of it.

Despite the latent feeling of anxiety in my chest, I open my Bible. I read, trying to focus exclusively on the words.

"As a deer pants for flowing streams, so pants my soul for you, O God."

But he hates m—

"My soul thirsts for God, for the living God. When shall I come and appear before God?"

When I appear before God, he'll conde—

"My tears have been my food day and night..."

I can relate to that.

"while they say to me all the day long, 'Where is your God?' These things I remember, as I pour out my soul: how I would go with the throng and lead them in procession to the house of God with glad shouts and songs of praise, a multitude keeping festival."

I used to happily lead others in glorifying God too.

"Why are you cast down, O my soul, and why are you in turmoil within me? Hope in God; for I shall again praise him, my salvation and my God."

Give me hope.

I'm not his child anymore, though.

It's worth trying.

I put down my Bible before any more thoughts intrude. I pick up my journal and my pen.

"God, I haven't been honest with you, nor do I think I possess the capability to. The notion that I must have a certain appearance before you is irrevocably ingrained in me. It seems beyond anyone's power to change.

I'm scared. I know what's inside me is sinful, and I'm afraid to let you see it. So, I put up a mask. I masquerade in front of everyone, including you. I'd like for you to think I have it all together—that I'm your perfect child. But I don't have it all together. I'm a Pharisee, although I don't want to be. I don't want to be prideful enough to think I have it all together. Help me.

Give me the faith to believe. Take my pride away. I don't like living like this. I'm terrified of you, even though I know I shouldn't be. I'm so afraid."

I set my pen and journal on my desk, and I turn out the light.

This journaling puts my mind at ease a little bit.

The usual debate turns in my head for about 15 minutes, and then I fall asleep.

Chapter 6

I walk into the lobby, check in, and sit down. Almost immediately, the door opens and my counselor steps out.

She smiles. "Hi, Ross. Come on in."

I walk through the door and into the same room as last week.

"How are you today?" she asks as I sit on the couch.

"I'm all right."

"Let me pray and we can get started."

She prays for a productive session and for God to heal me.

"Okay. So, how were you this past week?"

"Um, a little better. I mean, overall things haven't really changed. However, it was good to finally start this process last week. I don't know; just finally doing something I know I've needed to do for a long time is freeing."

"Absolutely. You've already taken the first and perhaps biggest step. You admitted you need help and you came in for it."

"Journaling has helped as well. I'm introverted and I express myself best through writing. I think it'll be a good thing to keep doing."

Her eyes show a bit of excitement. "Great! I was about to ask about that. How often did you do it, and do you think it's helped you express yourself to God?"

"I did it a couple times this week. I think it's helped. It's hard for me to express myself to God. I keep wanting to hide the bad from him. I want him to see all the good parts and none of the bad. It's hard to be honest with him."

40

She looks at me intently. "God doesn't accept you based on how well you're doing. He knows everything about you—the good and the bad—and he accepts you anyway."

I shake my head in frustration. "I feel like he's mad at me. I feel like I have to be some great saint for him to be happy with me. I know the concepts of God's grace in my head, but my heart doesn't accept them. It continually tells me I have to work for God to be pleased. It continually tells me I'm not good enough."

"It sounds like you need the knowledge in your head to connect with your heart. You need your heart to accept the doctrines and knowledge of God's grace that you know in your head."

I nod. "Yes. It's not easy. I try. I try to tell myself that I don't need to work for God's approval. I implore myself to believe it. But my heart is too used to operating under works. It's very frustrating. I tell myself all this truth, but it won't take." I run my hands through my hair as sort of a tick of frustration. She starts speaking and I look back up at her.

"It's going to take time, but you're on the right track. Ask God for faith. Ask God to change the operating philosophy of your heart. Like I said last week, read the Psalms and pray along with them for faith. Write those prayers down. One thing you can do as well is make a table. On one side, write what your feelings say is the way God sees you. On the other, write the truth of the gospel regarding how he sees you. Pray that you'll believe what the gospel says."

Tears are about to come from sheer frustration—frustration that somehow I can't accept that God loves me, that he's pleased with me, that he doesn't need me to be perfect. Ashamed, I hold back my tears and nod in response to her. She gives me a few moments. I take a deep breath and regain my composure.

"Have you made any decision about medication?"

"No. I don't know what I want to do yet."

"Okay. Do you have any friends who know what's going on?"

"Yes. I have a roommate who does. I've told him about pretty much everything. He knows I'm going to counseling."

"Great; that's a huge blessing. How about your parents?"

"They know I'm struggling. I talked to them before starting counseling because I thought we'd have to pay. I think they're confused about what's going on. They don't understand how I was doing so well and then dropped off a cliff, so to speak. But they're very supportive."

She nods. "Great. Is there anything else on your mind that you need to talk about today?"

I think for a moment. *Tell her about blasphemy against the Spirit.* I shake my head. "No, I don't think so."

"Okay. If you have any questions during the week just email me. I'll pray and you can go."

She begins praying, but I don't hear anything because I'm so frustrated with myself.

Why can't I bring this up? She's a counselor; it's not going to take her by surprise. She can help.

I...I just can't do it. It's so bizarre. I shouldn't be bothered by it. I just need to get over it.

"In Jesus' name, amen."

"Amen."

We both stand up and she opens the door for me.

"Thank you," I say as I leave.

"See you next week."

I nod.

Help me to say what's on my mind, God.

***

I turn off the overhead light, turn on my lamp, sit in my bed, and grab my pen and journal. Ever since my counseling session I haven't been able to stop thinking about my works-based approach to God.

I wish I could just click a button and it would go away. No matter how many times I pray or tell myself grace-based truth, this mindset won't leave.

I open up my journal to vent my frustrations.

"Somehow over the past four years I developed the idea that God is mad at me because I'm not good enough. I think I have to be better to meet his approval. The more I read theology the more I feel I'm not good enough or don't know enough. I would never admit it to anyone, but it's the way I think.

I've believed for a long time that God is angry at me, but I've never told anyone. My happiness in him has diminished. I've become depressed and withdrawn. I've dug myself deeper into a hole, although I've hid it behind books, schoolwork, and mission. I've replaced God with mission, theology, and acceptance from others. Once these pillars I've hid under collapsed, I was exposed."

I turn the page. On the top left-hand side, I write "How I Feel." On the top right-hand side, I write "What the Gospel Says."

On the left side under the title, I write, *"Rejected. God is displeased with me."*

43

On the right side under the title, I write, "*I am saved by grace through faith in Jesus.*"

On the left I write, "*Cast out. God won't take me back. Alone. If I don't get my life together, God won't accept me.*"

On the right, "*My salvation is based upon the work of Jesus, not my performance. I am God's child; he will never leave me or forsake me.*"

On the left, "*Beyond his forgiving grace.*"

On the right, "*My sins are completely forgiven.*"

On the left, "*God has bigger and better things to attend to than me. He doesn't care about my soul.*"

On the right, "*He loves me with everlasting love.*"

I immediately turn to the next page and start writing my prayer.

"*God, I don't believe you. I want to believe your every word— to embrace it, cherish it, and love it—but my heart refuses. I'm lonely, and it feels as though you've forsaken me. But your word promises you won't.*

I'm hurting. I should have dealt with these issues long ago, and now I feel like you're mad at me. I want to feel your love again. I don't want to think I have to 'be somebody' for you to accept me. I want to believe you love me in spite of me. Help me believe, whatever it takes.

I confess that I studied your word and prayed for the sake of others and not my own relationship with you when I led Bible studies and Christian groups. While I was serving you, I forgot you. Forgive me, and never let me repeat my mistake."

My eyes are closing. I set my pen and journal on my desk, turn off my light, and place my head on my pillow.

***

I pull up in the lot of my friends' apartment and park. I walk down the walkway, up the stairs, and knock on their door.

"Hey! What's up, man?" my friend Kevin says as he opens the door.

"How are you doing?" I ask.

"Good, man. We got food already on the table. Come on in and take a seat."

I walk in towards the table. "Wow. I don't even have to wait?" I say jokingly.

"No, it didn't take as long as we thought it would."

I walk towards the table and see Dan in the kitchen.

"What's up, Ross? Glad you could make it," he says.

"Yeah. Thanks for cooking. Sure looks good," I say as I survey the food.

Dan laughs. "Well, let's hope it tastes good."

Kevin casually swats the air by his face as if to dismiss the thought that the food could taste badly. "Dan's a good cook. It'll be fine."

"Grab a drink and let's eat," Dan says to me.

I pour myself some water and we all sit at the table.

"Where's Nate?" I ask.

Kevin does a half eye roll. "He's on the phone with his girl. He'll be out soon."

We pile food on our plates and start eating.

"How's the internship going?" Dan asks.

"Not bad. I'm helping coach a football team as part of the church's sports outreach. I wish I was a little more involved, but that's okay," I respond.

"I bet some of those kids are tough to deal with, huh?" says Kevin.

I shrug. "Yeah. Many of them come from a rough background. Overall, I like them. They're good kids; they've just had a rough go at things."

"How's counseling going? I don't think I've talked to you since you started," Dan says.

"It's going well. It's not easy working through issues, but I know it's a process. I just tell myself to keep praying and keep working at it. We'll see what happens from there. I do wish things would progress faster."

"Just keep at it. You'll see results. We're praying for you," Kevin says.

"Yep. What he said," Dan says with a good-natured laugh.

I smile in response to Dan. "Thanks. I appreciate it."

We discuss some church issues and then talk sports. As we finish eating, Nate walks out of his room.

"Glad you could join us!" Kevin says with mock excitement.

"Hey!" Nate says with a smile. "Sorry. I got a little caught up on the phone there."

I say hi to Nate with a good "bro" handshake, and he sits at the table.

"Grab something to eat," Kevin says, motioning to the food on the table and in the kitchen.

"That's okay. I'll get some later," Nate replies nonchalantly.

"Okay. Well, we said we were going to have a little prayer meeting. So, maybe we should do that before watching sports or a movie," Kevin declares.

"Let's do it," Nate says.

Kevin puts his hands together as if he's planning. "So, how about each person talks a little about what they'd like prayer for or who they'd like to pray for. Then, the guy to his right can pray for him/his requests. I'll start and Nate will pray for me."

Kevin talks for a minute and we bow our heads as Nate prays for him. We listen to Nate as he talks, and then I pray for him. It's my turn.

"As y'all know, I'm going through counseling. During the first few weeks I've learned how much of a works-based approach I take to my relationship with God. Basically, I don't think he loves me or accepts me if I'm not doing enough good works for his kingdom. So, I think he's mad at me all the time."

Tell them about blasphemy of the Spirit.

There's a knot in my throat. I hesitate.

"A few months ago, I randomly had involuntary blasphemous thoughts against the Holy Spirit. Normally, I don't think I would've thought anything of it. But at the time, I was struggling getting involved on campus, and because of that I already felt God was mad at me for not doing enough for his kingdom. So, I started engaging the thought and tried to convince myself I hadn't committed the unpardonable sin. But I thought God was already mad at me, so I succumbed to thinking I did it. For the past two months or so, I've been terrified I'm going to hell forever and there's nothing I can do about it. I try and convince myself otherwise, but for some reason I can't. The thought won't go away. So, a big part of my counseling is learning to truly believe the gospel in my heart. If y'all could pray for that, that would be great."

"For sure," Dan says, and he launches into prayer. It wasn't easy, but I'm relieved I said something.

We finish up prayer and turn on sports. We sit and chat for a while and Kevin turns on a movie. About thirty minutes in I look at my phone and see that it's late. I say bye and walk out to the parking lot. I feel a slight sense of release—almost a feeling of freedom. Encouraged, I jump in my truck and drive to my apartment.

Chapter 7

I still don't feel great, but I've made a bit of progress. I'm actually opening up some. That gives me hope. I told my counselor last week that I opened up to my friends in prayer time. I still didn't tell her about the unforgivable sin. I wanted to, but it didn't come out. So, I still have some work to do. I think I should try medicine. I think it's the next step. If I want to get as well as I possibly can, I need to at least try it. If it makes me feel worse, I'll get off it.

I pray about it for a minute; then, I think of next steps. *I'll tell my parents tomorrow and then schedule an appointment.*

***

After discussing my plans over lunch with my parents, I pull up to my apartment, walk inside, and call my doctor. The receptionist answers and asks what she can do for me.

"I need to schedule an appointment," I say.

"Okay. And what will we be seeing you for?"

"I want to see about getting on medication for depression and anxiety."

She lists off available dates and times. I choose one.

"Sounds good. We will see you then," she replies.

"Thank you."

I set down my phone and breathe a deep sigh. I'm a little nervous, but hopeful.

***

I turn off the overhead light, turn on my lamp, grab my laptop, and sit on my bed. I research a few things about depression medication, just to know what to expect. I place my laptop back on my desk and go out to the living room and kitchen to do my nightly checks before bed. I check the front door locks, the stove, and the oven. Right when I'm about to head back to my room, my roommate, who is on the couch, says, "Dude, what are you doing?"

"I'm about to go to sleep. I'm just making sure this stuff's off."

He straightens an arm at me with his palm up. "You've been checking that stuff for like five minutes. You should get your OCD checked out."

"What?"

He laughs. "Do you not realize how OCD you are? You check that stuff over and over every night and every time you leave."

I'm dumbfounded. I've been checking locks, stoves, ovens, electrical outlets obsessively for years, and it never once considered it was Obsessive Compulsive Disorder. It got really bad after the onset of my depression; I just assumed it was part of my depression.

"I never realized it was OCD."

"I thought you knew. How could you not know? It's obvious! I didn't think I had to say anything about it for you to know!"

I raise my eyebrows and nod my head once in agreement. "Yeah, I guess that's pretty obvious."

"But seriously, get some help for that. When I was little, I had some problems with it, but my mom took me to therapy and I got better."

I can't tell if he's joking about the last part. But either way, I know he's right.

"How did you not know?" he asks while laughing.

I can't help but smile. I can't believe I've been this oblivious. I shake my head. "I honestly have no idea."

I walk to my room, still shaking my head. I'm tired, and I don't want to stay up much longer, but I open my laptop again and research Obsessive Compulsive Disorder.

Checking locks, stoves, ovens repeatedly...if the person doesn't perform checks, he or she may fear something bad will happen to him/her or family...excessive worry about germs and/or diseases...intrusive violent, sexual, and/or blasphemous thoughts, and excessive worry about or surrounding those thoughts.

"Yep, I'm totally OCD," I whisper to myself.

I don't suffer from every symptom listed on this website, but there's no denying I'm OCD. So, I've been struggling with depression and OCD all these years, and I thought it was just depression. Everything makes a lot more sense. This unforgivable sin hang up came from my OCD. I need to get counseling for OCD.

I shake my head as I close my laptop and put it on my desk. I feel relieved now that I have a new understanding about myself. Thankfully I'm too tired for my mind to be racing. I pray and crawl in bed.

***

The door opens. "Ross?" the nurse says.

I stand up and walk over to her. "Hi, how are you today?" she asks.

"Good. How are you?" I respond.

"I'm doing well, thank you. Head over to the scale and I'll get your height and weight. Take off your shoes first."

I slip off my shoes and stand on the scale. She writes down my weight, asks me to step over to my right and place my back against the wall. I follow her direction and wait as she measures my height.

"All right. Grab your shoes and we'll be in the first room on the right."

She closes the door as I come in and I take a seat on the patient bed.

"I'm going to take a few measurements here," she says as she prepares her equipment. She places a pulse oximeter on my finger, reads my temperature, and then opens up the blood pressure cuff. I'm nervous; I know my blood pressure is high. Constantly thinking you're going to hell forever doesn't do much for blood pressure.

I look up at the meter. *Shoot.* My nurse asks if traffic was bad or if I've been stressed lately.

"Yes, I've been stressed."

She doesn't inquire further. She types in a few things on the computer and tells me the doctor will be in soon.

"Thank you," I reply as she walks out.

I gotta get that blood pressure down.

I wait for a few minutes, and my doctor opens the door.

He reaches out to shake my hand. "Hey, Ross. How are you doing?"

"I'm fine," I say as I shake his hand.

It's been a long time since I've seen him, so we shoot the breeze for a minute. I tell him about graduating high school, going off to the small college freshman year, and returning home to the large university.

"All right. So, you're here about depression and anxiety. When did this start?"

"It started my sophomore year of high school."

"What are your symptoms? Tiredness, sadness, trouble sleeping, can't get out of bed, tearfulness, loss of concentration, loss of interest?"

"Pretty much all the above."

"Okay. Have you had a drug or alcohol problem or a recent break up?"

"No."

"Have you taken anything for this or have you gone to counseling?"

"I haven't taken anything. I started counseling about a month ago."

"Good. Have things gotten better?"

"A little bit, yes."

"But you're still experiencing symptoms and want to try medicine?"

I nod. "Right."

He takes a deep breath, as if indicating he's about to speak for a while. "Usually with my depression patients I do Wellbutrin.

53

More often than not it helps, and it doesn't mess with your liver or kidneys or anything. Usually patients end up taking it for life if they have chronic debilitating depression. Some people just need it to make it through a tough time and then they're off. Depending on how this goes, we can reevaluate in a year or two and determine if you want to stay on it. I'm going to start you off on a lower dose to see how it feels. We'll meet again in two weeks to check in. If you experience any problems, email me or give me a call. It may make you feel weird at first, but it should even out and help you feel better within a week. I recommend taking it every morning after eating. Some people say it makes them feel more awake, so I wouldn't take it at night. How does all of that sound?"

"Sounds good to me."

"Great," he says as he writes a few things. "They will give you your prescription order when you check out." He shakes my hand. "Take it easy, man. I'll see you in two weeks."

"Sounds good. Thank you."

I walk out the door behind him and go to the check-out desk. I schedule my next appointment, receive my prescription order, and pay a small co-pay.

"You're good to go. Thank you," the receptionist says.

"Thank you," I respond.

I walk to my truck, get in, and head in the direction of the pharmacy.

***

My head feels fuzzy. I come into my room after taking a shower and sit on my bed.

I need to journal. I need to take care of myself.

I pick up my journal and pen and begin writing. My roommate walks in wearing workout clothes.

"Hey man, you want to come to the gym with me?"

I give him an incredulous look. "It's 10 p.m. I just took a shower. I'm going to sleep soon."

"All right. I just wanted to see. I know you're on that medicine and it made you feel funny the other day. I thought exercise might help."

"Yeah, you're probably right. I mean, I'm not going tonight, but I'm glad you said something about exercise. It's been a few days since I went to the gym. I'll go tomorrow."

"How have you felt today?"

"Not great. My head's been fuzzy all day. I can barely concentrate on anything. If this keeps up I'll call my doctor."

"Was it like this yesterday?"

"Well, to be honest, I didn't take it yesterday. I took it for the first time two days ago and it made me feel weird, so I just went without it yesterday. I took it again this morning hoping it would feel better on the second try."

"All right. Well, let me know how it goes in the next few days."

"Okay."

He takes a book out of his backpack and sets it on his desk. He glances at me as if he forgot something. "I gotta tell you real quick about this weird girl at the gym yesterday. You know the blue mats at the back? There's barely any space on them to begin with, and she kept hogging one of them..."

What if the medicine stays this way? What if it doesn't make me any better? I'll be destined to a life of exhaustion, constant involuntary mind-racing, tearfulness, and sadness.

I realize my roommate's still telling his story. I'm looking right at him, but my mind is flipping around constantly.

Pay attention.

"At this point, I'm pretty frustrated because I'm done with the rest of my workout and I need the mat to do the..."

I'm going to need to call my doctor if this keeps up. I can't handle this mind racing. It's noticeably worse than before. This medicine isn't—there I go again. C'mon, pay attention.

"I'm literally walking over to the mat. I'm a few steps away from it and she walks in front of me and plops down on it..."

I really want to pay attention to you, dude, but I can't right now. I'm sorry.

"Anyway, it was strange, and I hope she's not there again tonight."

"Yeah, dude, I don't know why someone would do that," I say, figuring some generic sympathy would suffice.

"Yeah, I agree. It makes no sense. I'll see you later," he says as he walks out.

I stare at the wall where his face was a few seconds ago. *This medicine better work soon.* I shake my head quickly as though I were shaking off distracting thoughts. I look back at my journal and write again.

***

I think I'm working myself into a panic. I couldn't focus on a simple conversation last night, and after taking the medicine again this morning I feel the same. Deep breaths in and out. Just keep going.

I've felt the anxiety in my chest all day. I'm trying my best to keep it at bay. I've never had a panic attack, and I don't want to start now, especially since I'm driving. *Deep breaths...deep breaths...deeeeeep breaths.*

The anxiety is slowly shooting upward from my chest to my head. *Hold it at bay for me, Jesus. Deep breaths, deeeeeep breaths. Thank God I'm almost there.*

I keep breathing deeply while I turn right into the shopping center. I drive around to the restaurant and park.

Thank God I can be out of the truck.

I walk in and find Kevin. He looks up at me from his phone. "Hey man, what's up?" he says.

"Hey. How are you?"

"Oh, not bad. Dan just told me he's not going to make it. Oh well, guess it's just you and me."

"That's all right. Who needs him anyway?"

He looks down at his phone again. "I'm texting him now. I'll tell him you said that."

I shrug. "Go right ahead."

Kevin sends the message and then grabs the menu. "Have you ever been here before?" he asks me.

"No."

"It's surprisingly good. You know, for somewhere that kind of looks like a hole in the wall."

"Awesome." I pick up the menu and browse.

After a few seconds we both put down our menus. "You know what you want?" Kevin asks.

"Yeah. I'm getting one of those shrimp dishes. They look good."

"Good choice."

We sit in silence for a few seconds. We're good friends, but neither one of us are big talkers.

Kevin breaks the silence. "So, how are things since the last time I saw you?"

"Eh, they're all right. I went to my doctor and got prescribed an anti-depressant. Today's my fourth day since I started taking it, although I've only taken it three of those four days. I gotta be honest, I don't think I've ever felt this bad. My doctor told me this might happen, but he said it should even out and start working within a week. I hope it does. My mind's been racing like crazy, I can't concentrate on anything, and I feel like I'm about to have an anxiety attack, which has never happened to me before."

"That sucks, dude. Sorry to hear that. I had some friends from high school who I never would've guessed had depression. But they told me they did. I was close to one or two of them; they told me they basically experienced the same thing when they started their medicine. But they said it helped them feel better shortly after that."

"Well, that makes me feel better. I don't know anybody who's had to go through this, so I didn't know what to expect."

The waitress walks up and takes our orders.

"Well, let me know if there's anything Dan and I can do to help," Kevin says as our waitress walks off.

"Thanks. I appreciate that. Just hanging out with you guys helps. Takes my mind of things a little bit."

58

"Good. That's what we're here for."

We talk sports for a while. Our food arrives and we switch to church issues. We finish up, say goodbye, and head to our trucks. I turn on my engine and head to the shopping center's exit. As I turn left at the light, I feel the anxiety returning.

I hate being alone. It's the worst when I'm alone. I need to surround myself with friends these next few days.

The anxiety clamps down on me. I do my best to take deep breaths and keep my mind from wandering. That's when it goes to dark places. Thankfully, my anxiety isn't as bad driving home as it was driving to the restaurant.

***

My roommate and I walk out of the library, grab our bikes from the bike rack, and start walking down the sidewalk. It's dark outside, but we just got through a few hours of reading and we're in a talking mood, so we walk with our bikes.

"What are you thinking about church? I know you've been considering moving to a new one," he says.

"I did some research and I'm going to try a small church that's right on campus this Sunday. Everyone who knows anything about it says it's great. I'll give it a try. I'm just tired of going to such a huge church where I never seem to feel connected. And it's not that I haven't tried. You know that. I just finished an internship there, and I've gone there for years and been involved in lots of different stuff. I've made friends there, but they're just kind of scattered here and there, except for you, Kevin, Dan, and Nate. I think a smaller church would suit me better, especially since I'm so introverted," I reply.

"Yeah, I understand. I think I might end up switching to a smaller church soon too."

I was looking straight ahead, but now I look over at him in surprise. "Really? Why?"

"Well, my youth pastor from the church I grew in is planting a church right now. It's just two miles away from our apartment. I talked to him about it a few days ago, and I think I'm going to start going there."

I focus in front of me again. "Oh, cool. Sounds like a good opportunity."

"Yeah. Let me know how you like the church Sunday. I hope you like it."

"I'll let you know."

We take a left turn at the bottom of the hill, cross the street, and walk on the sidewalk in the direction of our apartment.

"Are you going to do OCD counseling?"

"So, the church I'm visiting this Sunday has a counselor. I read about him online. I'm going to see about scheduling an appointment with him soon."

"Cool."

We walk in silence for a minute.

"Is your medicine still making you feel like crap or is it better now?" he asks.

"I had dinner with Kevin last night, and that's the worst I've felt since I started taking it. Today, though, I haven't noticed it as much. It hasn't been as bad. Granted, it's not making me feel great yet, but this is an improvement."

"Good. You looked kinda out of it a few nights ago."

I laugh. "I was."

Chapter 8

The same nurse from two weeks ago opens the door. "Ross?" she says.

I stand up and walk to her.

"Hi, how are you?" she asks.

"Good. How are you?"

"I'm doing well. I'm going to have you step on the scale there just like you did last time."

I walk to the scale and slip off my shoes. She takes my weight and my height again, and we head to the room. I sit on the bed as she readies the equipment. After my oxygen, heart rate, and temperature readings, she wraps the blood pressure cuff around my arm.

"Any traffic on the way here?" she asks as she pumps air into the cuff.

"A little," I respond.

She reads the meter and releases the air.

That was a little better. Still too high, though.

She types into the computer and then stands up. "He'll be right in," she says.

"Thank you."

A few minutes later the door opens and my doctor walks in. He immediately reaches out to shake my hand. "Hey, Ross. How are you doing today?"

"Not bad. How are you?"

"I'm fine. So, how did it go these past two weeks?"

"At first, it made me feel worse. But after a few days, it slowly made me feel better."

"Good. It does that. Were you consistent taking it?"

"Yes. I skipped one day at the beginning. That's it."

He nods. "Good. If you're okay with it, I'm going to increase the dose. I started you out with a fairly small dose. Let's see how this bigger does feels. If it helps you feel better, I think we'll keep it there."

"Sounds good."

He makes a note and looks back up at me. "Great. I'll get that prescription order ready for you. Let's meet again in two weeks to make sure everything's going all right. If you need anything, call or email."

"Great. Thank you."

"All right, Ross. See you in two weeks," he says as he shakes my hand.

We both walk out and turn in opposite directions. I walk to the check-out counter, schedule another appointment, get my prescription order, and pay the small co-pay. I thank the receptionist, walk to my truck, and start in the direction of the pharmacy again.

***

I grab my bike, close my apartment door behind me, walk down the steps, and start pedaling towards the gym.

My head feels a little stuffy, but this is much better than when I started the medicine two weeks ago.

I knew exercise would clear my head and I can already feel it. I cruise down a hill, enjoying the breeze.

I still don't feel as relaxed as I would like to, but this is certainly better than a few months ago when I couldn't get my mind off hell, even when I exercised. Now, the unforgivable sin and hell sit at my front door and keep knocking, but I don't let them in nearly as much.

I pull up to the gym, place my lock around my bike and a bike rack, and head inside. After checking in, I throw my stuff in a locker and head upstairs to the basketball court. I came at a good time; there aren't many people here. Thankfully, someone left a basketball, which I pick up and start shooting.

I'm willing to bet this stuffiness in my head will disappear after a few days of taking the higher dose. I just need to exercise through the next two or three days.

I resolve to come to the basketball court every day until the stuffiness disappears. I shoot around for 15 minutes by myself, and then a girl and two guys ask me to play a game with them. As we play, I can still feel the stuffiness.

This is annoying. I'd like to concentrate on the game, not my head.

My teammate passes me the ball and I take it to the basket for two points.

I've experienced worse, but this is still annoying.

I focus on guarding the offensive player. He passes.

C'mon, mind. Focus on the game.

The game soon ends. We shake hands and disperse. I walk down to the locker room, grab my stuff, and walk out. I'm a little annoyed at myself for focusing too much on my thoughts, but my focus has improved since two weeks ago and I know it'll get better.

***

The apartment door opens and closes. I hear several thuds and banging noises as my roommate sloppily maneuvers his bike past the table and into our bike corner. I stop reading and set down my book; I know he's going to come into the room talking about something. He opens the bedroom door.

"Hey, man, what are you doing tonight?" he asks.

"You witnessed the extent of it. Sitting and reading."

"Cool, cool. You want to grab dinner?"

"Yeah, sure."

"Cool. Is the regular spot okay?"

"Fine with me."

"All right. Give me a second and I'll be ready."

I turn off my desk lamp, change shirts, and put on my shoes. While my roommate puts his stuff up, I walk to the living room and check the stove and oven. A few moments later, he walks out. "You ready?" he says.

I take my eyes off the stove and look at him. "Yeah."

I turn around and follow him out the door. *Was it off?*

I look back inside before closing the door. My roommate is already walking off toward the parking lot talking. He doesn't notice I'm still at the door. I squint at the stove again.

That burner is off, that one's off, that one's off, that one's off. The oven...yep, it's off.

I start closing the door.

64

Is it all off?

I stop right before the door is shut.

Yes, it's all off.

Sure?

I checked it.

I force myself to close the door and lock it. I jiggle the handle and start walking towards the parking lot. My roommate is way over by the steps to the lot looking back at me; he must've gone all the way there before realizing I wasn't with him. When I get over to him he resumes where he left off. We step in his car and he starts driving.

Was everything off? Did I lock the door?

Yes, I know I did.

He continues talking.

Am I sure? Did I really lock the door? What if I didn't and someone steals our stuff?

Well, they wouldn't get much.

I manage to concentrate on my roommate for a moment.

I need to think about the do—

I focus on my roommate's story.

"Anyway, man. I haven't really been able to talk to you since Sunday. How did you like that church?" he asks.

Think about the do—

"I liked it. It's a small church; seems like it has a great atmosphere. The people were very friendly. Some guy sat down next to me and started a conversation. We talked before and after the service for a while, and he invited me to a small

65

group. I liked the preacher a lot too. I'm definitely going back next week. I think this could be a great fit for me."

"Nice. I'm glad to hear that. Seems like I've met a few people who attend that church, but I can't remember their names. I hear good things about it, though."

"Yeah. So far so good. I'm also going to schedule an appointment with the counselor there soon."

"Good stuff. Let me know how things are going with this church in the next few weeks."

"Yeah, I will."

We pull up to the restaurant, jump out, and are seated inside. Right when we sit, my OCD starts again.

Is the door locked?

I let it go.

As we start snacking on chips and salsa, we discuss a few of the classes we're going to have to take the next two semesters. After we order and we're about a third of the way into our meal, my roommate asks about my medicine.

I swallow and take a drink. "I feel so much better than a few weeks ago when I started. The first two days on the higher dose my head felt stuffy, but it doesn't now. I, like...I actually think the medicine is working. I think I'm feeling better."

"Great! I'm so happy you're feeling better, man," he says looking at me straight in the eyes to express how genuine he is.

"Yeah, me too. It feels like it's been so long since I haven't felt completely awful. I wasn't sure if it would ever happen. I mean, it's been at least over six months since everything got so bad with my depression and OCD. It's been such a long process."

We finish dinner, pay, head back to the car, and drive to our apartment.

I actually didn't obsess over the lock. I was able to eat dinner and converse like a normal person. And the last time I thought about blasphemy of the Spirit was this morning. I've almost gone a whole day without thinking about it.

I can't help but crack a little smile.

Chapter 9

I walk up to the door of the church, a little nervous, but not as bad as when I first went to depression counseling a few months ago. I peek inside the window and see my counselor coming to open the door.

He opens the door. "Hi. Ross?"

"Yes." I shake his hand.

"I'm David. Nice to meet you."

We walk up the stairs as we start some small talk. "Right over here," David says as we get to the second story. I follow him into the room and he closes the door. "Have a seat on that sofa there."

"Did you get a chance to fill out the paperwork I emailed you?" he asks.

"Yes, sir. I did," I reply as I take out the papers from my backpack and hand them to him.

He peruses them for a moment. "Okay. So, you went in for depression counseling a couple months ago?"

"Yes, sir."

"On a scale of one to ten, how bad would you say your depression was when you began counseling?"

"Probably an eight."

He nods. "What would you say it was when you finished the counseling?"

I think for a moment. "About a six."

68

"Okay. So, it helped?"

"Yes."

"And you say on here that you just began medication around a month ago."

"That's correct."

"How has that made you feel?"

"Bad at first. But now it's made me feel better. It's made a positive difference."

"Good. So, that's helped your depression even more?"

"Yes, it has."

"Great. Sounds like you're on the right track. So, you're coming in for OCD counseling, correct? Have you ever completed counseling for OCD?"

I shift in my seat and set my backpack on the floor. "Yes, I'm here for OCD counseling. No, I've never done counseling for it. I didn't know I had it until a month or so ago."

"Have you done any research on it?"

"Some, yes."

"What sort of symptoms do you experience?"

I shift my eyes to the wall while I think about what I read. "I check my stove, oven, and locks a bunch before I sleep or leave my apartment. I also have intrusive nasty thoughts about God that bother me. Those are the two that bother me the most."

"Okay. So, those bad thoughts about God are obsessions. Checking the stove, oven, and locks—those are compulsions. What do you mean by nasty thoughts about God? What kind of images or thoughts about him come into your head?"

69

I feel myself wanting to hesitate, but I make myself spit it out. "Calling him Satan."

"And why exactly does that bother you?"

"I...I feel like God's mad at me for saying that. I feel like he won't forgive me for it."

He looks intently at me. "Son, there's nothing you can do to separate yourself from God's love. He died for all your sins. Having intrusive thoughts calling him Satan isn't going to separate you from his love."

I nod. "I know that in my head. I try to tell myself that, but I still find myself worrying about it."

Talk about the unpardonable sin.

"I...I know this may sound ridiculous—"

"Nothing is ridiculous in here," he immediately interjects.

I nod again. "I worry about the unforgivable sin. That maybe I committed it when intrusive thoughts came in calling God the Devil. I mean, I literally blasphemed the Holy Spirit in my head. The thought popped up sort of randomly one day, and it's bothered me since."

"Have you read Romans?" he asks without pause.

"Yes, sir."

"Paul says in Romans that he is convinced nothing will be able to separate us from the love of Jesus. No sin—nothing. Not even calling the Holy Spirit bad names in your head."

I nod. "I know that. I try and tell myself that, but the thought won't go away and I obsess over whether or not I did it."

"That's what I'm going to teach you how to manage in the next few sessions. When you feel like you have to think about the

70

unpardonable sin, or you feel like you have to touch the stove again. We're going to work on some strategies and breathing exercises to help you move past your obsessions and compulsions."

He hands me a few stapled sets of paper. I briefly scan them.

"Read through these articles before our next session. Practice the exercises they talk about. We'll discuss them in depth next time."

I quickly slip the papers in my backpack and look up at him. "Sounds good."

"Let me pray."

He prays, we say goodbye, and I walk down the stairs and out the church door.

***

My nurse opens the door and smiles at me. "Come on back, Ross," she says.

I perform the regular routine. Shoes off, on the scale, off the scale, shoes back on, into the room. As I sit on the bed, she asks, "Was traffic bad?"

"No, I think this is the quickest I've gotten here."

"Good," she says as she takes my vitals. When she starts my blood pressure, I look up at the meter.

Okay. Making progress.

"The doctor will be right in," she says as she puts the cuff away and leaves.

After a few minutes, he opens the door, and we exchange our routine handshake and greeting.

"All right. So, how did thc higher dose feel?"

"The first two days were a little funky, but after that it was great. I could feel it making a difference."

"Great. That's what we want. I'm going to write you a 90-day prescription. We'll check in at the end of that time to make sure everything's still okay, which I imagine it will be. If it is, I'll give you a 90-day with one refill. So, we'll only see each other twice a year at that point. Like always, if you need anything, just let me know."

"Great. Sounds good."

He smiles and shakes my hand. "All right. I'll see you then. Sorry to make you drive for such a short visit."

I laugh. "No big deal."

I head to the check-out desk. After performing my normal check-out functions, I get in my truck and head to the pharmacy.

***

I throw my backpack over my shoulder and walk to the door. I stop in the living room and take a deep breath.

Check the burners once, breathe. Check the oven once, breathe, and be done.

I look over at the burners. *That's off...breathe, breathe, breathe...That's off...breathe, breathe, breathe...That's off...breathe, breathe, breathe.*

I finish and turn to the door.

Were they off?

Don't check. I already did. Breathe, breathe, breathe.

Without turning, I open the door, walk out, and lock it. I jiggle the handle. *It's locked. Breathe.*

I turn and walk to the parking lot. As I start driving, I feel the anxiety approach.

It's off and locked. Breathe, breathe.

I drive the short drive to the church. I hop out of my truck with my backpack. *The lights are off, it's in park, both doors are locked.* I close the door behind me and walk to the church door. Just like last time, David is waiting and opens the door for me.

"Hey Ross. Good to see you. How are you doing?"

"I'm doing well. How are you?"

We walk up the stairs to the same room. I sit on the couch again. We bow our heads and David prays.

After we lift our heads David asks, "Did you get a chance to read those articles?"

"Yes, sir. I did."

"What did you think?"

"I thought they were very informative. I didn't know anything about Cognitive Behavioral Therapy or breathing exercises."

"Those articles do a great job explaining. Have you tried the breathing exercises?"

"Yes. I used them on the way over here." I ignore the small, silly wave of pride that comes over me.

He smiles. "Great! Does it make a difference?"

"Yes, it does."

"Great. Just keep practicing them. It'll get easier as you continue. Did it work better with your obsessive thoughts or compulsions or both?"

"It worked very well for both. When I started thinking about blasphemy against the Spirit, I just focused on breathing for five or so seconds and let the thought go."

He nods vigorously. "That's what we want."

We practice the breathing technique together for a few minutes and discuss some smaller points of the articles. At the end of our time, David asks me to pray. I then say goodbye and walk back to my truck feeling a new sense of calm and freedom I haven't felt in years.

Chapter 10

I walk out of the church door, onto the sidewalk, and turn right. I had some business on campus earlier this morning, went to counseling, and now I'm going back on campus for another errand. I walk down the sidewalk towards the street, turn right, and walk a few more yards to the crosswalk. A few other students wait with me for the light to change. I look behind me at the large façade of the old Baptist church that neighbors my church. I'm not sure why I'm looking at it besides the fact that it's a beautiful building. The large trees next to it provide shade to the church doors.

I look intently at the tree that almost hugs the building's right side. Something's different about it. The leaves exude more color, the intricate details of the bark are more noticeable—the whole tree seems more alive.

I notice the students start crossing the street. I turn away from the tree and follow them. As I walk, I feel a strong sense of joy. I think of the counseling session I just came out of. It was my last session with David.

"I actually feel like I have control over my OCD. I'm not sure if I've ever felt that way in my life. Even when I was a kid and my symptoms would pop up, I didn't really have control. I just found ways to distract myself. I didn't know it was OCD back then; all I knew was I worried a bunch. I have a lot more confidence now. I know I can deal with this however it reveals itself in the future," I said.

"And remember, you can only praise God in the present," David said. "Don't get so caught up in what you did that wasn't perfect or something coming up that you're nervous about. You can only praise God in the present."

I nodded.

"Okay. I think I've done all I can do for you right now," he said cheerfully.

I glance around at the surrounding large oak trees that provide shade for the campus walkways, protecting myriad students from the sweltering Texas summer sun. For the first time in years, ever since my depression came around five or six years ago, I feel a sense of normalcy. Everything doesn't feel so grey, dull, lifeless. I can concentrate on the present. I can focus on the beauty of my surroundings without distraction. I can *live* in the present.

How long has it been since this horrible time with my OCD and depression started? When was it that I started thinking about the unpardonable sin all the time?

I do some calculations in my head.

Not too far off from a year. It took me almost a year to feel better. Honest to God, I wasn't sure if it was ever going to happen. All the fighting, the clawing, the scratching to feel better...it was worth it. If I had to, I'd do it all over again. It was worth it that much.

I reach the fountain by the street. Students walk in all directions like ants. I try and hide my small smile. Don't want them to think I'm crazy.

Afterword

"I wish I had never written many of these despondent words. But I did. Thank God he has made me more mature, joyful, and hopeful since then. 5/2/13"

After filling up my small journal with scribbled prayers during a hard year of Obsessive Compulsive Disorder and depression, I wrote the above three sentences on the front page and dated it. I finally felt better, and one day not long after my last OCD counseling session I looked through my journal.

I was almost ashamed at some of the things I wrote. I was embarrassed. Was I really that desperate? But I knew I had been. Still, a part of me wanted to throw the journal away or cover it up and say none of it ever happened.

It's hard to tell people about your mental health struggles when you want them to view you as a strong, godly person. It's just hard in general to open up about mental health problems. You think people are going to look at you funny, you think they probably won't understand. They might say some vague, almost confused comment about how they're happy you feel better (because thank God you're better—I wouldn't know what to say to you if you weren't better).

I can't really blame people, though. Someone who's never experienced depression or anxiety or OCD or bi-polar disorder doesn't know what it's like. How would they? That's not their fault. I do think, though, that our society needs to get better at listening to people with mental health issues, being there for them, supporting them at every turn, and in some instances standing up for them. I think there's a just-get-over-it or it's-just-a-season mentality many have, which is extremely detrimental to those truly struggling. Mental health is kind of a taboo subject—just ignore it and maybe it'll go away. We need to be able to be honest, and we need to be able to talk openly.

I was blessed to have two different roommates during my difficult year who provided much-needed support. They didn't judge, they didn't ignore, they didn't try to fix me. They made it known they were there for me, they asked me how I was doing but didn't pry, they got me out of the "bat cave" that was our apartment, and they made me laugh. I'm extremely thankful for them—more than they know.

It really did take me a year to feel better. Just a month after finishing OCD counseling, I met the girl who would become my wife at my new church. We started dating that August, got engaged exactly a year after our first date, and got married nine months later. She has given me so much joy—joy I didn't think I'd ever feel during the year prior to us meeting.

I also worked at my new church the summer I met my wife. Throughout my time leading college group Bible studies and participating in various other activities there, I found tremendous joy. There's much joy in serving God and serving others. My wife and I also moved to Colorado shortly after our wedding. We've experienced incredible outdoor activities and the beauty of the Rocky Mountains. All that to say this: I'm incredibly happy to be alive. All the time and effort I put in to feel better during that year has been completely worth it.

Granted, I was never suicidal. There were many points in the years of my depression and OCD that I wanted to die. But as those who've felt the same can attest, there's a difference between that and being actively suicidal.

I guess I'm trying to say this: I hope this book helps someone, somewhere, in some point in time. Perhaps that person has struggled with some of the same things I've described. I was not suicidal, but that person may be. I want that person to know that there's hope in Christ Jesus. There's hope you'll come out of this and live a better life than you ever thought possible. Just keep going, just keep praying. You never know how God might surprise you.

About the Author

As a son of a military man, I was born in California, lived in Europe as a small child, and attended grade school in Texas. My wife and I currently live in Colorado, where we love to hike with our two dogs, paddle board, fish, and snowboard.

You can check out all my writing and receive a free book download on my website: www.wrhwriting.com

Other books by W.R. Harris:

The Pincushion Heart

Thoughts on American Evangelical Culture

Made in the USA
Middletown, DE
11 May 2020

Fear of irreversible eternal damnation..
God seems absent...

This is the true story of a young man's obsessions and compulsions.

HEALTHY HOMEMADE
DOG FOOD
COOKBOOK & GUIDE

70+ BALANCED MEALS

Transform Your Dog's Life and Discover **Healthy, Natural, Nutritious, Easy-to-Make** Recipes

HELEN SUTHERLAND